POLAR ANIMALS
DICTIONARY

An A to Z of polar creatures

Author Clint Twist
Editor Elise See Tai
Art Editor Julia Harris
Art Director Miranda Kennedy
Cover Designer Arvind Shah
Production Director Clive Sparling
Consultant Zoologist Valerie Davies
Illustrators Richard Bonson (The Art Agency), Robin Boutell
(The Art Agency), Myke Taylor (The Art Agency), Gill Tomblin.
Andromeda Children's Books would like to apologize in advance
for any unintentional omissions.

Created and produced by
Andromeda Children's Books
An imprint of Alligator Books Ltd
Gadd House
Arcadia Avenue
London N3 2JU
UK

This edition produced in 2007 for Scholastic Inc.
Published by Tangerine Press, an imprint of Scholastic Inc.,
557 Broadway, New York, NY 10012

Scholastic and Tangerine Press and associated logos are trademarks
of Scholastic Inc.

ISBN-10: 0-439-89813-7
ISBN-13: 978-0-439-89813-3

Printed in Malaysia

Information icons

Throughout this dictionary, there are special icons
next to each entry. These give you more information
about each creature.

Maps

These maps appear next to each creature and will
show you whether the creature can be found in the
Arctic or Antarctic, or both.

Arctic   **Antarctic**

Size comparison pictures

Next to each entry you will see a symbol, either
a hand, an adult human, or a diver next to a red
icon of the creature listed. The symbol shows you
the size of each animal in real life compared to the
size of a human.

7 inches

The first symbol is a human adult's
hand, which measures about
7 inches (18 cm) from the wrist
to the tip of the longest finger.
Some creatures are smaller than
this, so this symbol helps you
to imagine their size.

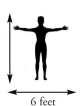

6 feet

The second symbol is an adult
human. The height of the human
is about 6 feet (1.8 m). With
arms outstretched, the arm span
measures about 6 feet (1.8 m).
This symbol helps you to
compare the height or length
of a creature to a human.

6 feet

The third symbol is an adult
diver. The length of the diver
measures about 6 feet (1.8 m)
from head to toe. This symbol
will help you to imagine the
length of some creatures.

POLAR ANIMALS
DICTIONARY
An A to Z of polar creatures

tangerine Press®

an imprint of

SCHOLASTIC

www.scholastic.com

The polar regions

The North and South poles are the northernmost and southernmost points on the Earth's surface. They are the places farthest from the equator and as a result, they get the least amounts of sunlight and the Sun's heat. These polar regions are cold places throughout the year, so cold that the sea is frozen solid and they are covered with snow. Despite these similarities, the North and South poles are very different places.

Arctic

The region around the North Pole is called the Arctic. It is defined by the Arctic Circle, which is about 66.5 degrees north of the equator and includes the northern parts of the continents of North America, Europe, and Asia, as well as the island of Greenland. These large masses of land enclose the Arctic Ocean. At the North Pole itself there is no land, just frozen seawater. In winter, the frozen sea allows land animals to move from one continent to another.

Arctic Circle

Asia

North America

Arctic Ocean

• North Pole

Greenland

Europe

Dall sheep

Arctic loon

Antarctic

The region around the South Pole is called the Antarctic. There is an Antarctic Circle, which is 66.5 degrees south of the equator. The situation here is the opposite of the North Pole. The Antarctic is defined by the continent of Antarctica and the surrounding Antarctic Ocean, which is sometimes called the Southern Ocean. Even in the coldest winters, the continent of Antarctica is always surrounded by liquid water, so land animals cannot easily move there even if they wanted to. Antarctica is the coldest and windiest place on Earth.

Polar environments

The polar regions are dominated by ice caps—vast areas of compressed snow and ice that are many hundreds of feet thick. In the Antarctic, there is little else except the ice cap, some mountains, and a rocky shoreline, much of which is permanently frozen. In the Arctic, however, the polar regions are parts of larger continents. The Arctic ice cap is surrounded by areas of ground that thaw in summer, and then by areas of coniferous forest.

Australia

Antarctic Circle

Africa

Antarctica

• South Pole

New Zealand

Antarctic Ocean

South America

Macaroni penguin

Antarctic cod

Polar animals

Life around the poles is very different from life elsewhere on Earth. Around the North and South poles, most animals on land are warm-blooded mammals and birds. There are no reptiles or amphibians, and there are very few insect species. The pattern to life here is very different from other places. The main reason for this is that there is a lack of food for herbivores because it is too cold for most plants to grow. Most polar animals are predators.

Chinstrap
penguin

Marine life

In the polar seas, there are fewer differences to life elsewhere, especially in the Arctic region. One big difference is that the polar seas have much greater numbers of marine mammals than other regions. One reason for this is that being warm-blooded helps survival in polar waters. The cold water is also rich in food for many creatures. Another reason is that the extreme climate deters most human hunters. The Antarctic Ocean is unusual because it has far fewer fish species than the other oceans, and the individual fish are on average quite a bit smaller.

Minke
whale

Thermal protection

Keeping warm is the key to survival for polar mammals and birds. Their bodies produce enough heat; the trick is not to lose this heat to the cold environment. Thick fur and feathers provide an insulating layer that traps air, prevents heat loss, and keeps the skin warm and dry. Beneath the skin there is usually a thick layer of insulating fat known as blubber. In the Antarctic Ocean, many fish produce natural antifreeze chemicals so that they can survive the freezing water.

Hooded seal

Migration

Another trick for polar survival is to avoid being there at the coldest times of the year. Many birds breed in the Arctic region during the summer and then fly to warmer places when the Arctic winter begins. This form of regular long-distance travel is called migration. On land, a few mammals, such as the caribou, migrate each year. In the polar oceans, some whales tend to migrate, while others, along with penguins and seals, do not.

Giant petrel

Seasonality

Although it is cold throughout the year, there is a big difference between winter and summer in the Arctic and Antarctic regions. In winter, everything is frozen, but in summer, some of the ice melts. In the Antarctic, it remains too cold for any plants to grow except for mosses and a few tufts of grass. In the Arctic, however, the melting snow and ice reveal large areas of grassy tundra, with a few dwarf trees.

Aa

Adelie penguin

Max height: 23⅗ inches (60 cm)

This small penguin is one of the very few animals that can survive in Antarctica throughout the year. During the brief Antarctic summer, the Adelie penguin nests around the coast on sheltered beaches. Each pair of penguins builds a roughly circular nest of pebbles to stop their eggs from rolling away.

Fact
In the 20th century, Alaskan king crabs were introduced to the North Atlantic where they have since become a menace to other sea life.

Alaskan king crab

Max length: 18½ inches (47 cm)

Also known as the red king crab, this large crustacean is found in the northernmost parts of the Pacific Ocean, around the coasts of Alaska, Japan, and Siberia. Weighing more than 22 pounds (10 kg) when fully grown, and equipped with powerful claws, the Alaskan king crab is the undisputed "king" of the ocean floor.

Antarctic cod

Max length: 5 feet (1.5 m)

The Antarctic cod, which is also known as the yellow-belly rock cod, is the largest of the 200 or so fish species that are found only in Antarctic waters. Its body produces special antifreeze chemicals that prevent it from freezing in the icy water.

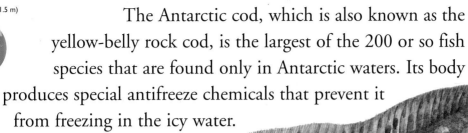

Arctic hare

Max length: 26 inches (66 cm)

The Arctic hare is found only in the treeless, open tundra of northern Canada and Greenland, although a very similar species lives in northern Siberia. It shelters from the icy winds in small crevices on rocky slopes. In winter, the Arctic hare has a thick coat of white fur, but in summer, its fur is thinner and much darker in color.

Aa

Max length: 36 inches (91.5 cm)

Arctic loon

The Arctic loon, which is also known as the black-throated diver, is a bird that spends almost its whole life on water. In summer, it lives on the many freshwater lakes scattered across the tundra of North America, Europe, and Asia. In winter, when the lakes freeze over, the Arctic loon moves out to the open seas.

Max length: 4½ inches (11.5 cm)

Fact
People once believed that the barnacle goose was hatched from a barnacle rather than from an egg like other birds.

Arctic warbler

The Arctic warbler is a small songbird that spends the summer feeding and breeding in the cold coniferous forests of northern Europe and Asia. Large numbers of Arctic warblers arrive in spring when insect prey becomes plentiful. In autumn, they migrate southward to spend the winter in the warm climate of Africa or India.

Max length: 10 inches (25.5 cm)

Auklet, crested

The crested auklet is a small seabird that nests in huge colonies around the coastlines and islands of the Bering Sea. It feeds on animal plankton and uses its wings to "fly" underwater as it chases after prey. During the breeding season, crested auklets attract mates by producing a peculiar tangerine-scented smell.

Max length: 27 inches (68.5 cm)

Barnacle goose

This waterbird can be distinguished from other geese by its pale face and the black and white stripes on its upper wings. In winter, it lives around the coasts of Denmark, Germany, and Britain. In summer, it migrates northward to Greenland and western Siberia for the breeding season.

Bb

Max length: 18 feet (5.5 m)

Beluga whale

This small whale is found only in the Arctic Ocean, where it often forms large groups around the mouths of rivers during the summer. The beluga is one of the most vocal whales. Its "songs" can be heard over some distance. It is sometimes called the sea canary because of the types of sounds—whistles and chirps—it makes.

Max length: 110 feet (33.5 m)

Max length: 17 inches (43 cm)

Black-legged kittiwake

The black-legged kittiwake is a gull that spends most of its life soaring above the open sea or resting on the water's surface. This bird comes to shore only during the summer, when it nests around the Arctic coasts of North America, Europe, and Asia.

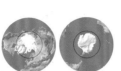

Blue whale

This marine mammal is the largest and heaviest animal on Earth. During the winter, the blue whale moves to warmer waters for breeding, while it spends the summer in the cold waters of the Arctic and Antarctic. Despite its enormous size, the blue whale feeds on krill that are only about ¾–2⅓ inches (2–6 cm) long.

Fact

The blue whale is sometimes called "sulphur-bottom" because algae growing on its skin can make its underside appear sulphur-yellow.

Max length: 10 inches (25.5 cm)

Boreal owl

This small owl is found throughout the cold, northern forests of North America, Europe, and Asia. The boreal owl usually nests in an old woodpecker hole in a tree and hunts only at night. This flying predator preys on both small mammals on the ground and small birds perched on branches.

Bb
Cc

Max length: 24½ feet (7.5 m)

Bottle-nosed whale

This little-known marine mammal is found only in the southern oceans. It may dive to depths of more than 3,300 feet (1,000 m) and can stay underwater for about an hour. In summer, it is often sighted close to the edges of the Antarctic ice.

Fact

Most bottle-nosed whales have only two teeth, which are located at the tip of the lower jaw.

Max length: 1 inch (3 cm)

Caddis fly

The caddis fly is a moth-like insect that spends most of its life as a larva in streams and lakes. The larva spins a protective tube of silk around its body to which it attaches fragments of plants, stone, and shell. Some caddis fly species live in pools on the Arctic tundra, where the larvae can survive beneath the winter ice.

Canada goose

Max length: 45 inches (114 cm)

This large waterbird is found throughout North America. It has also been introduced to parts of Europe and Asia. In summer, the Canada goose inhabits the tundra, taking advantage of the seasonally abundant food. In winter, it migrates in V-shaped formations, sometimes flying as far south as Mexico.

Caribou

Max length: 7 feet (2.2 m)

The caribou is found throughout Alaska and Canada, and also in northern Europe and Asia where it is known as the reindeer. The caribou is an herbivore and in summer, it feeds on the grass and shrubs of the tundra. In winter, it survives on moss and lichens, which it scrapes from rocks and trees.

Cc

Max length: 37½ inches (95 cm)

Char, Arctic

The Arctic char is a large freshwater fish that likes cold water and is found only in the most northerly parts of the world. It is related to trout and salmon. Most char migrate between rivers and the Arctic Ocean, but some remain in lakes throughout their lives.

Fact

Char are very popular with anglers and have been introduced into some waters for fishing. There are even some in a lake in New Hampshire, U.S.A.

Max height: 30 inches (76 cm)

Chinstrap penguin

The chinstrap penguin can easily be recognized by the distinctive black markings on each side of its head. It lives mainly on rocky, steep-sided islands off the coast of Antarctica. It uses its beak to help it climb up to its nest, which is sometimes as much as 328 feet (100 m) above sea level.

Max length: 2½ inches (6.2 cm)

Clouded yellow butterfly, northern

The northern clouded yellow butterfly lives on the Arctic tundra throughout the year. In spring and summer, it feeds on the many tundra flowers. In winter, it survives being frozen under the snow thanks to the thick hairs that cover its body.

Fact

Crab-eaters are the most numerous seals in the world because of the decline in the number of blue whales; fewer whales means more krill for the seals.

Max length: 8½ feet (2.6 m)

Crab-eater seal

This seal is found throughout the cold waters around Antarctica and around the southern tips of Africa and South America. It is a fast swimmer and can reach speeds of 15 mph (25 km/h) underwater. Despite its name, this marine mammal does not feed on crabs—it uses its teeth to filter krill from the water. Its coat is dark gray or brown during winter and blond in the summer.

Dd

Max length: 6 feet (1.8 m)

Dall sheep

This wild sheep lives in the mountains of Alaska and western Canada. It is closely related to the bighorn sheep, which looks very similar. The two species are often confused, but Dall sheep tend to be smaller and live in colder and more northerly regions.

Max length: 14 inches (35.5 cm)

Dominican gull

This seabird is also known as the kelp gull. It is the only gull that breeds in Antarctica, and it is restricted to the northernmost tip of the rocky Antarctica Peninsula. This gull sometimes feeds on krill or dead seals, but its main food is shellfish that live on the coastal rocks.

Fact
The Dominican gull got its name because early Spanish explorers thought the plumage on its head looked like the hood of a Dominican monk.

Max length: 4¼ inches (10.8 cm)

Dragonfly

In spring and summer, the wetter parts of the Arctic tundra are full of small flying insects such as mosquitoes. This abundance of insect prey attracts insect predators such as the subarctic darner dragonfly. These dragonflies are able to survive the cold tundra winters and feast on the millions of summer mosquitoes.

Fact

Dragonflies feed on mosquitoes throughout their lives. Dragonfly larvae (non-flying juvenile forms) live in water, where they prey on mosquito larvae.

Max length: 7½ inches (19 cm)

Dunlin

The dunlin, which is also called the red-backed sandpiper, is a small shorebird. When it is winter in the northern hemisphere the dunlin can be seen collecting food at the sea's edge in many parts of the world. In spring, it migrates back to its breeding grounds in northern Canada, Greenland, and Siberia.

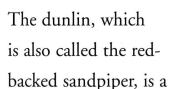
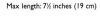

Dd

Ee

Max length: 20 inches (51 cm)

Eider duck

The eider is a sea duck that spends most of its time among the floating ice of the Arctic Ocean. It comes ashore only to nest on rocky beaches. The eider duck is kept warm in the icy Arctic waters by a thick layer of insulating feathers that also keep its skin dry.

Max length: 21 feet (6.5 m)

Elephant seal, southern

The southern elephant seal, which is found only in Antarctic waters, is by far the largest of all seals. A fully-grown male can weigh more than 5½ tons (5 tonnes). Male elephant seals have a thick, fleshy nose that can be inflated to impress females or frighten rival males.

Emperor penguin

Max length: 3.5 feet (110 cm)

This is the largest of all penguins. It can withstand the full force of an Antarctic winter, which is also the breeding season and when it lays eggs. When the egg is laid, the male stands and protects it on his feet under his stomach feathers through months of winter weather, in which temperatures go as low as -76°F (-60°C). During this time, the males lose about half their body weight as they cannot go to the sea for food.

Max length: 9½ inches (24 cm)

Ermine

Ermine is the name often given to the stoat in winter when its fur is pure white apart from a black tip on its tail. This small carnivore is found throughout North America, Europe, and northern Asia. The stoat hunts on the ground, and preys on lemmings, voles, and other small mammals. It will also steal eggs from bird nests.

Fact

Stoats only turn white in regions with extensive winter snowfall. In other places, they retain their brown fur throughout the year.

Eskimo curlew

Max length: 4 inches (10 cm)

The Eskimo curlew is probably now extinct—it has not been seen since the 1980s. These birds once migrated in large flocks from their summer breeding grounds in Alaska and the Canadian Arctic, to the grasslands of South America for the winter. A combination of hunting and habitat destruction has reduced these flocks to nothing.

Eurasian beaver

Max length: 39 inches (99 cm)

The Eurasian beaver lives near forest streams and rivers in northern Europe and northwest Asia. It is slightly larger than its relative, the American beaver, and has a different way of life. The Eurasian beaver does not gnaw down trees to build dams and lodges. Instead, it digs a burrow in the riverbank.

Max length: 72 feet (22 m)

Fin whale

The fin whale is the second largest of the whales. It is sometimes sighted in Arctic and Antarctic waters, but in general, it prefers warmer conditions and migrates to more tropical waters during the winter to breed. The fin whale uses fringed plates of baleen inside its mouth to filter krill, small fish, and other creatures from the water.

Max length: 22 inches (56 cm)

Fox, Arctic

This fox occurs in two distinct color types. The "white" fox has a thick coat of white fur for camouflage in snow and ice, but in summer, its fur is brown and only about half as thick. The "blue" fox tends to live in more shrubby areas and is pale gray/brown tinged with blue in winter.

Max length: 7½ feet (2.3 m)

Fur seal, Antarctic

The Antarctic fur seal is related to sea lions. It is an extremely agile swimmer that attacks schools of krill at high speed. These fur seals are mainly found on the island of South Georgia and on a few other remote islands off the coast of Antarctica.

Gg

Gentoo penguin

The gentoo penguin nests on Antarctic islands, and sometimes on the continent itself. This bird has a different fishing method from most other penguins. Adelie and chinstrap penguins swim far out to sea and make shallow dives in search of food. The gentoo stays close to the coast and dives deeper to search for food near the seabed.

Fact

Gentoos were once called tussock penguins because they build their nests among tussocks, tufts of grass, on Antarctic islands.

Max length: 37 inches (94 cm)

Giant petrel, southern

The southern giant petrel is a large seabird that is only found in the oceans around Antarctica. Although it sometimes feeds on squid and krill that it catches at the sea surface, the giant petrel is also a predator that attacks colonies of penguins. It walks through a colony of penguins, ignoring the adults, and takes chicks and young birds from their nests.

Glacier bear

Max length: 6¼ feet (1.9 m)

Glacier bear is the name given to the American black bear that lives in the ice-covered mountains of Alaska and western Canada. Although these large mammals are classified as carnivores, they obtain more than 95 percent of their food from plants, especially in the form of fruits and berries.

Greater snow goose

Max length: 28 inches (71 cm)

The greater snow goose has pure white plumage with black wing feathers. In summer, it nests on islands off the north coast of Canada and on the coast of Greenland. In winter, it migrates southward along the eastern coast of the United States. Snow geese sometimes gather in flocks of up to half a million birds when migrating.

Gg

Max length: 16 inches (40.6 cm)

Grouse, willow

The willow grouse is one of the few birds that live on the Arctic tundra throughout the year. The grouse spends most of its time on the ground, and in summer, it has brown feathers that blend in with the tundra's vegetation. In winter, its feathers become white to match the snow.

Fact

Red grouse, found only in Britain, are a species of willow grouse that do not turn white in winter.

Fact

More so than eagles, gyrfalcons were considered to be the birds of kings in Europe during the Middle Ages.

Max length: 23 inches (58.5 cm)

Gyrfalcon

This rare bird of prey, which is found only in the Arctic region, is the largest of all the falcons. It feeds on other birds and small mammals such as hares and lemmings. Some gyrfalcons have white feathers with black speckles, while others are a dark gray color with paler stripes.

Max length: 5 inches (12.7 cm)

Hoary redpoll

The hoary redpoll, which is also known as the Arctic redpoll, is a type of finch. It feeds mainly on seeds, especially from dwarf willow and birch trees. The hoary redpoll nests in summer in the northernmost parts of Siberia, Canada, and Greenland. Some stay in the Arctic throughout the year, while others migrate southward in winter.

Hh

Max length: 9 feet (2.7 m)

Hooded seal

The hooded seal is a marine mammal that lives in the North Atlantic around the coastline of Greenland. Only the males of this species have a "hood"— a fleshy muzzle that can be inflated to make the male's head seem twice as big. This hood is not a means of defense against predators—it is used to impress females and frighten rival males.

Hh

Max length: 5¼ inches (13.3 cm)

Horned lark

The horned lark, which is also known as the crested shore lark, nests in summer around the coasts of the Arctic Ocean. The distinctive "horns" on its head are a part of its summer plumage. In winter, when the horned lark migrates to warmer coastlines, it loses these feathered horns.

Max length: 6 feet (1.8 m)

Hourglass dolphin

This small marine mammal is found only in the cold Antarctic Ocean. It has distinctive black and white markings on its sides that on some animals look like an old-fashioned hourglass. This dolphin prefers the open sea instead of shallow coastal waters, and it is often seen swimming alongside fin and sei whales.

Hh Ii

Max length: 52½ feet (16 m)

Humpback whale

The humpback whale migrates back and forth across the world's oceans. In summer, it prefers to feed in cold polar waters, but in winter, it moves into warmer waters. The humpback is easily identifiable by its huge flippers. It is also the most acrobatic of the large whales and sometimes leaps above the water's surface.

Max length: 28 inches (71 cm)

Icefish

The icefish  is found only in the waters around Antarctica. It is a predator with sharp teeth that feeds on krill and smaller fish. The icefish is extremely unusual because it does not have red blood—its blood does not have the special red cells that give blood the red color.

29

Ii Jj

Max length: 17 inches (43 cm)

Ivory gull

This small gull spends its whole life in and around the Arctic Ocean. It is most often seen along the edges of the sea ice, where it feeds mainly on fish and shrimp. The ivory gull will sometimes follow polar bears at a safe distance, so it can feed on any scraps of meat that the bears leave behind.

Max length: 22 inches (56 cm)

Jaeger

Jaeger, which means hunter, is another name for the Arctic skua, a seabird that is related to gulls. The jaeger is a very unpleasant neighbor—it feeds on the eggs and young of other seabirds that nest nearby. It also steals food from other birds by ambushing them in midair.

Max length: 33 feet (10 m)

Jellyfish, lion's mane

Max length: 10 feet (3 m)

The lion's mane jellyfish is the world's largest jellyfish. The biggest specimens are found in the cold waters of the Arctic Ocean. Trailing beneath its blob-like body are about 1,000 tentacles. Each one of these is equipped with stinging cells that can inject venom into the jellyfish's prey.

Killer whale

This large marine predator is found in both Arctic and Antarctic waters. The killer whale is closely related to dolphins. It lives in a family group called a pod and hunts mainly large prey such as seals and other whales. In the Antarctic, the killer whale also preys on penguins.

Fact
Killer whales are very aggressive hunters that will sometimes try to grab seals that are at the water's edge.

Max height: 10½ feet (3.2 m)

Kodiak bear

Kodiak bear is the name given to brown bears that live on Kodiak Island near the coast of Alaska. These bears are bigger and fiercer than the grizzly bears in the Rocky Mountains. The Kodiak bear is the largest of all the various types of brown bear and can weigh more than 1,700 pounds (770 kg).

Fact
There are eight types of brown bear—grizzly, Kodiak, Alaskan, Eurasian, Syrian, Siberian, Manchurian, and Hokkaido.

Krill

Max length: 2⅓ inches (6 cm)

Krill are small, shrimp-like animals that live in the ocean. They often form huge swarms of millions of individual animals. Krill are the main source of food for many Antarctic animals, especially whales, penguins, and the misnamed crab-eater seal.

Lapland bunting

Max length: 6 inches (15 cm)

The Lapland bunting is also known as the Lapland longspur. It is a small sparrow-sized bird that lives on the ground and feeds on seeds and insects. In summer, it builds a nest of dried grass and moss on the treeless Arctic tundra. In winter, it migrates southward, generally to coastal areas.

Fact

As with many Arctic animals, changes in the weasel's coloring are triggered by changes in the amount of sunlight they receive.

Least weasel

Max length: 8 inches (20 cm)

The least weasel is the smallest of all the meat-eating mammals and can weigh as little as 1 ounce (30 g) when fully grown. It is widespread throughout North America, Europe, and Asia, and is found as far north as the shores of the Arctic Ocean. In winter, the least weasel's fur turns completely white.

Ll

Max length: 12 feet (3.6 m)

Leopard seal

This fierce predator is found only in the cold waters around Antarctica. Unlike most other seals, the leopard seal uses its front flippers for swimming. It hunts by making high-speed attacks on smaller seals and penguins. The seal seizes its prey in its mouth and then smashes the animal against the surface of the sea.

Fact

Leopard seals stay close to the edge of the permanent sea ice. They sometimes break through the ice to grab a penguin walking above.

Max length: 8½ inches (21.6 cm)

Little auk

The little auk, which is also known as the dovekie, nests in summer around the shores of the Arctic Ocean. It feeds on zooplankton, which it catches by diving into the sea, and uses its wings as flippers to swim underwater. The little auk spends its winters at sea, in the slightly warmer waters of the North Atlantic.

Max length: 17 inches (43 cm)

Long-tailed duck

The long-tailed duck is also known as the Oldsquaw. This small duck nests near the lakes and ponds that form on the Arctic tundra during the summer. The long-tailed duck migrates southward to spend the winter along the coasts of North America, Europe, and Northeast Asia.

Max length: 40 inches (100 cm)

Lynx, Canadian

The Canadian lynx is also found in Alaska. This medium-sized wildcat prefers a forest environment, but sometimes ventures onto the tundra. In winter, the lynx's fur turns white and the fur on its paws becomes thicker, which makes it easier for the animal to walk over soft snow.

Mm

Macaroni penguin

This small penguin has a distinctive tuft of yellow feathers at each side of its head. The macaroni penguin nests in large colonies on remote islands in the southernmost parts of the Atlantic and Indian oceans. There may be as many as five million macaroni penguins in a single colony.

Max height: 30 inches (76 cm)

Merlin

Max length: 12½ inches (31.7 cm)

The merlin, which is sometimes called the pigeon hawk, is a small bird of prey. In summer, it nests on the ground on the Arctic tundra, and migrates southward in winter. The merlin mainly preys on small birds that it catches in midair when they are close to the ground. It will also hunt for voles and lemmings.

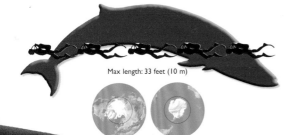

Max length: 33 feet (10 m)

Minke whale

This medium-sized whale can be found throughout the world's oceans. It tends to gather in polar waters during the summer months. The minke whale is much smaller than its close relative, the blue whale, but it feeds on exactly the same food—krill and other zooplankton.

Fact

An adult moose weighs more than 1,700 lb (800 kg) and eats about 77 lb (35 kg) of vegetation per day in summer, but only 33 lb (15 kg) per day in winter.

Max length: 11½ feet (3.5 m)

Moose

The moose, which is also known as the elk, is the largest of all deer. It lives in small groups in Arctic forests and on the tundra. In summer, it is often found near lakes and streams where it feeds on water plants. Males have distinctive antlers that are used for contesting with other males.

Mm

Max length: ¼ inch (7 mm)

Mosquito

People normally associate the mosquito with warm, tropical regions. However, the Arctic tundra can be one of the worst places in the world for these tiny, blood-sucking insects. The lakes and pools that form on the tundra are a perfect breeding place for mosquitoes.

Fact

Adult female mosquitoes suck blood, but they do not eat it. They need certain substances contained in blood in order to produce eggs.

Max length: 5¼ feet (1.6 m)

Mountain goat

This sure-footed animal lives in the mountains of western Canada and southern Alaska. It has sharp-edged hooves with a soft pad in the middle. The sharp edges help the hooves to grip on icy surfaces and the soft pads prevent the mountain goat from slipping on patches of bare rock.

Mm Nn

Max length: 7½ feet (2.3 m)

Musk ox

Despite its name, this large Arctic mammal is more closely related to sheep than to cattle. It lives on the tundra throughout the year, protected from the winter cold by its long, thick coat. If threatened by wolves, a herd of musk oxen will form a defensive circle around their young.

Max length: 14¼ feet (4.5 m)

Narwhal

This highly unusual whale is found only in the cold waters of the Arctic. The male narwhal has a tooth that grows into an elongated, spiral horn. This horn is not used for hunting prey as the narwhal mainly eats small fish and squid. Scientists believe the horn is used for contesting with other males in the same way that male deer use their antlers.

Nn Oo

Max length: 6 inches (15 cm)

Norway lemming

The Norway lemming is one of several lemming species that live on the Arctic tundra. This small plant-eating mammal is related to rats and mice. In winter, the lemming makes tunnels beneath the snow so that it can feed. In summer, it nests in underground burrows.

Fact

In years when summer conditions on the tundra are especially good, the number of lemmings increases dramatically. These are known as "lemming years."

Osprey

Max length: 23 inches (58.5 cm)

This bird of prey is sometimes called a fish eagle because fish are its favorite food. In summer, the osprey nests near streams and lakes on the tundra, and also around the ice-free Arctic coastlines. In winter, it migrates as far south as North Africa and Mexico.

Max length: 19 inches (48 cm)

Peregrine falcon

The peregrine falcon, which nests throughout most of the Arctic region, is the world's fastest-flying bird. It preys on other birds that it swoops down to catch in midair with its sharp talons. On the tundra, the peregrine falcon sometimes nests near colonies of red-breasted geese, which it ignores as prey.

Fact
A peregrine falcon can fly horizontally at about 100 mph (160 km/h). It reaches a speed of more than 200 mph (320 km/h) when it dives.

Max length: 22 inches (56 cm)

Pintail duck

The pintail duck is found throughout North America, except for the northeastern region, and also across Europe and northern Asia. In summer, it nests as far north as the shores of the Arctic Ocean, and migrates southward for the winter.

Pp

Pp

Max length: 11 inches (28 cm)

Plover, golden

The golden plover is a ground-dwelling bird that nests on the Arctic tundra. The golden speckles on the upper side help camouflage it from birds of prey flying overhead. In summer, the feathers of the underside are black, but they turn almost white in winter.

Max length: 20 inches (51 cm)

Plunder fish

The plunder fish is found only in the cold, deep waters of the Antarctic Ocean. Like most other Antarctic fish, it does not grow much more than 20 inches (50 cm) long, and its body produces natural antifreeze chemicals. Plunder fish spend most of their time resting on their fins on the seabed.

Polar cod

Max length: 15¾ inches (40 cm)

The polar cod is found only in the North Atlantic and Arctic oceans. It is related to the Atlantic cod, although it is much smaller in size. It feeds mainly on small shrimp-like animals that live beneath the ice surrounding the North Pole.

Pycnogonid

Max length: 19¾ inches (50 cm)

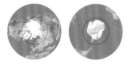

The pycnogonid is an unusual animal that is often called a sea spider, although it is not closely related to the spiders that live on land. Most pycnogonids grow to only a few inches in size, but in the cold Arctic and Antarctic waters, they grow much larger.

Rr

Raven

Max length: 25 inches (63.5 cm)

The raven is a type of crow, but it can withstand much colder temperatures than any of its close relatives. It is found throughout the Arctic region in North America, Europe, and Asia. In mountainous areas, the raven nests at heights of up to 20,000 feet (6,000 m)—well above the snowline.

Fact
Ravens like to eat animals that are already dead. They will peck flesh from the bones of animals killed by other predators such as wolves.

Razorbill

Max length: 17 inches (43 cm)

This seabird nests in summer around the Arctic coasts of eastern Canada, Greenland, and northern Europe. It spends the winter at sea in the North Atlantic. The razorbill uses its wings as flippers to swim underwater and catch fish in its knife-shaped beak.

Max length: 26 inches (66 cm)

Red-breasted goose

This rare waterbird nests in summer on the Arctic tundra of northern Asia. Some colonies of red-breasted geese allow peregrine falcons to nest among them. The falcons help protect the colony from hungry Arctic foxes in search of eggs or chicks.

Max length: 14 inches (35.5 cm)

Rock ptarmigan

This ground-dwelling bird lives on the Arctic tundra throughout the year. In summer, it has a speckled brown coloration, but in winter, its feathers turn white except for the tail and those around the eye. The rock ptarmigan is a major source of food for falcons and owls.

Rr

Rr

Ross's gull

This Arctic seabird, which is identifiable by its black neck ring, nests along the northern coasts of Greenland, Alaska, and Siberia. It spends the winter at sea and is rarely seen farther south than Iceland. Ross's gull swoops down to catch shrimp and small fish at the sea surface.

Max length: 13½ inches (34.3 cm)

Rough-legged buzzard

Max length: 22 inches (56 cm)

This bird of prey, which is sometimes described as a hawk, nests on the Arctic tundra during the summer months. The rough-legged buzzard hunts by hovering in midair and then swooping down to grab voles or lemmings in its sharp talons.

Max length: 33½ inches (85 cm)

Salmon, sockeye

Salmon are one of the few fish that migrate between freshwater and seawater. The sockeye salmon starts life in Arctic rivers such as the Yukon River. It spends most of its adult life in the North Pacific, but later returns to the same river in order to breed.

Ss

Max length: 4¼ feet (1.3 m)

Sea otter

The sea otter is the world's smallest marine mammal. It is completely adapted to life at sea and only rarely comes ashore. The sea otter lives in the northernmost parts of the Pacific Ocean, especially in offshore kelp beds. Some sea otters live as far north as the southern coast of Alaska.

Fact

Sea otters eat shellfish that they break open on a stone while floating on their backs at the ocean's surface.

Ss

Max length: 17 inches (43 cm)

Sheathbill, snowy

The snowy sheathbill lives on some Antarctic coasts, especially near colonies of penguins. The sheathbill is a scavenger—it feeds on penguin droppings, takes penguin eggs, and sometimes steals food from the mouths of penguin chicks.

Max length: 48 inches (122 cm)

Siberian white crane

This beautiful and rare bird nests in summer in only two remote regions of the Siberian tundra. In winter, it migrates to southern China and northern India. Siberian cranes are extremely shy birds and will not allow humans to approach nearer than about 1,300 feet (400 m).

Snowshoe hare

Max length: 23½ inches (60 cm)

The snowshoe hare, which is only found in North America, is often mistaken for the Arctic hare. Both animals have a white winter coat, but the snowshoe hare has shorter ears and is more of a forest animal, although it occasionally strays onto the tundra. Its summer coat is brown.

Fact

The main predator of the snowshoe hare is the Canadian lynx. In years when the number of hares increases, so does the number of lynxes.

Max length: 28 inches (71 cm)

Snowy owl

The snowy owl lives in the Arctic throughout the year. It has thick white plumage to insulate it from the cold. It even has feathers over its nostrils at the sides of its beak. The snowy owl hunts mainly small mammals, but will also take birds as large as ducks.

Ss

Max length: 1/16 inch (2 mm)

Springtail

The springtail is a small, wingless, plant-eating animal that is found almost everywhere on earth, including Antarctica. It is just about the largest land animal to live year round on the continent of Antarctica. The polar springtail can survive being frozen to -60°F (-50°C) without suffering any damage.

Fact

Springtails have six legs and were once classified as wingless insects, but scientists now think springtails are in a class of their own.

Squid, colossal

Squids, which usually come to the surface only at night, are widespread throughout polar waters and provide food for many other animals. However, the colossal squid, which lives in the Antarctic Ocean, is one of the largest and most fearsome predators on the planet.

Max length: 40 feet (12 m)

Max length: 8 feet (2.5 m)

Steller's sea lion

This is the largest of all sea lions—it lives in the Bering Strait and along the Pacific coasts of Canada and Siberia. Although it is protected by thick fur, Steller's sea lion cannot tolerate the colder waters of the Arctic Ocean. It can dive to depths of more than 650 feet (200 m) in search of fish, and it also hunts seals near the surface.

Ss
Tt

Tern, Arctic

Max length: 15 inches (38 cm)

The Arctic tern is probably the most traveled bird in the world. It nests along Arctic coasts in the spring and then flies across the globe to the shores of Antarctica. After taking advantage of the Antarctic summer, it then flies back to the Arctic. The tern feeds during its migration by diving into the sea for fish.

Tt

Thick-billed murre

Max length: 16½ inches (42 cm)

This seabird, which is also known as Brunich's guillemot, is related to auks. It nests on cliffs along the Arctic shores of western Siberia, Europe, Greenland, and eastern North America. The thick-billed murre feeds mainly on fish, which it catches while swimming underwater.

Timber wolf

Max length: 5 feet (1.5 m)

The timber wolf—also known as the gray wolf—is the largest of the wild dogs. Once widespread throughout the Arctic region, it is now found only in the most remote areas. Timber wolves hunt in packs of 10 to 20 animals, and will attack prey as big as caribou and musk oxen.

Max length: 4 feet (1.25 m)

Trout, Arctic lake

Trout belong to the same group of fish as salmon and char. The Arctic lake trout lives in deep, freshwater lakes in the Arctic regions of Alaska and Canada. It survives the winters near the lake bottom beneath the ice. The lake trout can live to be 40 years old, by which time it can weigh 120 pounds (55 kg).

Fact

Trout are difficult fish to classify—even expert scientists are not sure exactly how many trout species exist. Arctic lake trout are in fact a species of char.

Max length: 9 inches (23 cm)

Turnstone, ruddy

The ruddy turnstone is a small shorebird that nests along the northern shores of Alaska, Greenland, and Siberia. It feeds on small animals that it picks out from seaweed. At the beginning of the Arctic winter it migrates southward, with some birds flying as far as Australia.

Uu
Vv

Max length: 11½ feet (3.5 m)

Ursus maritimus

The polar bear's scientific name is *Ursus maritimus*. It is found throughout the Arctic region and is the only large land animal that can survive in an environment with no vegetation. The polar bear is a fearsome predator that feeds mainly on seals, sometimes breaking through ice to get at its prey in the water beneath.

Max length: 5¼ inches (13.3 cm)

Varying lemming

The varying lemming, which is also known as the northern collared lemming, is found on the tundra in the Arctic regions of North America. It gets its name because in winter its fur turns completely white. The varying lemming is the only rodent in the world (out of more than 1,700 species) to do this.

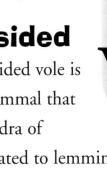

Vole, gray-sided

The gray-sided vole is a small mammal that lives on the Arctic tundra of Siberia. The vole is related to lemmings and is active throughout the year. In winter, the gray-sided vole tunnels under the snow in search of seeds. It is one of the main food sources for many small Arctic predators.

Max length: 4¾ inches (12 cm)

Max length: 13 feet (4 m)

Walrus

This unusual marine mammal is found only in the cold waters of the Arctic Ocean. The walrus is related to seals and sea lions, but it has long tusks, which are actually extended upper teeth. Only the males have tusks. Walruses form large breeding colonies on Arctic coasts, and they feed mainly on shellfish.

Ww

Wandering albatross

Max length: 63 inches (160 cm)

This large seabird spends most of its life gliding above the cold waters of the Antarctic Ocean. It swoops low over the sea to grab squid from just below the surface. The albatross only breeds about once every three years. There is a single chick, which the parents have to feed for up to nine months.

Weddell seal

Max length: 9½ feet (2.9 m)

The Weddell seal lives farther south than any other mammal on Earth. While other Antarctic seals stay in the regions of seasonal sea ice, the Weddell seal prefers to stay where the sea is permanently frozen. It uses special teeth that protrude from the jaw to dig breathing holes up through the ice to the surface.

Whistling swan

Max length: 5 feet (1.5 m)

The whistling swan is also known as Berwick's swan. This large waterbird nests in summer on the Arctic tundra of Alaska, Canada, and Siberia. In winter, it migrates southward to the coastline around Britain and to the northeastern and western coasts of the United States.

Whooping crane

Max length: 54 inches (137 cm)

If you are lucky enough to see a whooping crane, it is easily recognizable by the bare red skin on its head. This extremely rare bird nests in just a single location in the Arctic region of Canada. In the middle of the 20th century there were just 15 of these birds in existence, but numbers have since increased to about 250.

Fact

Whooping cranes have a wingspan of more than 6 ft (2 m). They fly south to spend the winter in southeastern Texas.

Ww

Max length: 4 feet (1.25 m)

Wolverine

The wolverine is one of the fiercest predators of Arctic tundra and forests. This mammal is related to weasels and stoats, but is much larger. The wolverine sometimes waits on tree branches to ambush migrating caribou as they pass below. A wolverine can kill a caribou with a single bite to the back of its neck.

Max length: 13 feet (4 m)

Wood bison

The wood bison is now found only in remote Arctic forests in northern Canada. It was once more widespread, but its numbers have been much reduced by hunting. The wood bison is larger and more hairy than its more familiar relatives, which live on the American plains, and has a longer neck.

Yy Zz

Yellow-nosed albatross

Max length: 30 inches (76 cm)

Although it is smaller than its wandering relative, the yellow-nosed albatross is no less powerful as an ocean flier. It is usually sighted far from land, soaring above the South Atlantic and swooping down to the surface to seize fish in its beak.

Fact
The yellow-nosed albatross is so-named because of the yellow ridge on its beak.

Zooplankton

Max length: 1½ inches (4 cm)

Zooplankton is the name given to the number of small marine animals that drift on the ocean currents. Some animals, such as krill, are plankton throughout their lives. For others, being plankton is just the first part of their life cycle. Zooplankton is a vital source of food for many sea creatures.

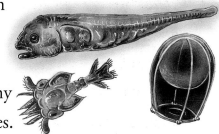

Glossary

Amphibian An air-breathing animal with a backbone that lays its eggs in water. Frogs and toads are the most commonly encountered types of amphibian.

Antarctic Relating to the region around the South Pole.

Arctic Relating to the region around the North Pole.

Baleen Plates of bristly mouth-bone used by some whales to filter food from seawater.

Bird A warm-blooded animal that has a body covered with feathers and that lays hard-shelled eggs.

Bird of prey Any bird that hunts and eats other birds, mammals, reptiles, amphibians, or fish.

Carnivore An animal that eats the freshly-killed bodies of other animals.

Colony A large number of animals of the same species, which live crowded together in a small area.

Coniferous Describes trees with thin, needle-like leaves that grow in cold climates. Most coniferous trees are evergreen—they do not lose their leaves in winter.

Continent One of the large landmasses that are surrounded by the seas and oceans.

Crustacean A type of multi-legged animal that is found almost exclusively in the sea. Crabs, shrimp, and lobsters are all crustaceans.

Equator A geographical line around the middle of the Earth. Conditions near the equator are almost the opposite of polar conditions—it is always very warm and often raining.

Flippers The front legs of dolphins, whales, and seals, which have developed into flattened projections from the sides of the body.

Glossary

Freshwater Rainwater, river water, and the water in most lakes is called freshwater because it contains no salt.

Glacier A river of ice moving very slowly downhill from an ice cap.

Habitat The combination of landscape, climate, vegetation, and animal life that forms the natural environment for a particular species.

Herbivore An animal that feeds on plants.

Ice cap An area of land permanently covered by a thick layer of snow that has been compressed into solid ice.

Insect A small, six-legged animal that does not have a backbone and which often has wings.

Insulation A substance that reduces the transfer of energy such as heat or sound.

Jellyfish A boneless animal with a nearly-transparent body and long, stinging tentacles.

Kelp Seaweed that grows long strands anchored to the sea bottom. Along some coasts, kelp forms "forests" that attract many sea creatures.

Larva (larvae is plural) The juvenile or young form of an insect, which changes its appearance when it becomes an adult.

Lichen One of a group of plant-like organisms that grow on tree bark and the surfaces of rocks and stones.

Glossary

Mammal A warm-blooded vertebrate animal that produces live-born young. Most mammals are covered with hair and live on land. There are a few marine mammals, such as seals and whales.

Marine Describes anything to do with the seas and oceans.

Migration Regular movement of animals from one place to another. Some birds and whales migrate thousands of miles each year.

Predator An animal that hunts and eats other animals.

Prey An animal that is hunted and eaten by others.

Reptile A cold-blooded animal with a backbone, which breathes air and produces live young, hard-shelled eggs, or eggs with leathery shells. Crocodiles, lizards, turtles, tortoises, and snakes are all reptiles.

Rodent One of a group of small mammals that includes rats, mice, and squirrels, but not rabbits or hares.

Scavenger An animal that feeds on the bodies of animals that are already dead, and other types of waste.

Plankton Tiny plants and animals that float in water and provide food for many sea creatures.

Polar Relating to the regions around the North and South poles.

Seabird A bird that spends some or all of its time flying over the open sea.

Seaweed Plants that spend all or part of their time submerged in seawater.

Glossary

Tundra An area of windswept, open landscape in polar regions. The ground is frozen solid for most of the year, but the spring thaw allows short grasses and other plants to grow during the brief summer.

Vegetation All the plants—from mosses to trees—that grow on a particular piece of land. The term is not normally used for plants that grow underwater.

Shellfish A non-scientific term for sea creatures, such as crustaceans and some mollusks, which have a hard outer shell.

Shorebird A bird that lives along coastlines, but does not venture far out to sea.

Species The particular scientific group to which an individual animal (or plant) belongs. Each species is a unique design and has a two-part scientific name. Members of the same species all share the same characteristics and differ only slightly in color or size.

Tropical Belonging to the geographical region around the equator, between the Tropic of Cancer and the Tropic of Capricorn. The tropical climate is usually hot and rainy.

Warm-blooded Describes mammals and birds, which are the only animals that produce their own individual body heat.

Waterbird A bird that spends some or all of its time close to freshwater rivers, lakes, and marshes.

Index